Opinions
and Testimonies

Opinions
and Testimonies

Marcus Robinson

STUDIO
OF BOOKS
THE SPACE FOR YOUR MESSAGE

Studio of Books LLC
5900 Balcones Drive Suite 100
Austin, Texas 78731
www.studioofbooks.org
Hotline: (254) 800-1183

Ordering Information:
Special discounts are available on quantity purchases by corporations, associations, and others. For details, contact the publisher at the address above.

Printed in the United States of America.

ISBN-13: Softcover   978-1-964148-58-8
              eBook   978-1-964148-59-5

Library of Congress Control Number: 2024910879

Table of Contents

MY MESSAGE FROM GOD

W ould you ever look at it? Like you're on an assignment. To be the best version of yourself. Bringing out the best of several to limitless people. I stand on the facts. To live is also to believe. There's good and bad in everything. Awareness is the best way to travel to your destination. Listen to yourself. What do you really hear? Not the second or third voice. The first inner voice. If it's good judgment. Why should you debate it?

Love is Power

The measure of Trust changes like the sands in an hourglass. If given enough time. That could be Good or bad. A Blessing or a curse. Trust bonds to love's foundation. Love is a powerful statement. It's the main action the Lord tells us to take towards one another. But if you don't believe in God, how could you ever love an outsider? I guess it's the same as if you don't love yourself. What can anyone else do for you?

A Simple Message

To those that think you're nobody, you're somebody. Just ask anybody who loves you. Sometimes you have to have a perception of reality. If there's a room full of evil people, What do you really think is going to happen? When No love exists in the room. You can't feel comfortable. It would be a better world. If people value others for the good in them. Lives are ruined because of the bad attacks. It rises out of the shadows. No mercy.

Judge not

To the Bigots, Hypocrites, & Plain ole chumbuckets trying to be an influence with their dead end knowledge of this life. They can be judgemental to whoever they want, daily. But hopefully no one's praying to get into "their" heaven. Minding your own business has declined tremendously everywhere! Live and let live unless it's a problem that directly affects you! God deals with everyone. In correct timing. And if you're not God fearing. You still know that you have a date for the end of your existence. Why waste time judging someone? Unless you're trying to put that person in a mental jail. It happens all the time. But there's all types of professional help for that. I recommend the almighty God. That's my opinion!

Being human

Somedays you might not be feeling a person. Maybe you're stressed or just want to isolate yourself for peace of mind. (who hasn't felt that way?) You can have love for everyone. Even if you don't show it on some days. If there is mutual love between you and that person. There's no love lost. And on those days, just ask for forgiveness. In prayer. No one is perfect. In fact, most people choose to hide their imperfections. Would rather put on a show. Appearing to be strong. I'm sure that it's quite tiring. Which probably creates mood swings and stress. Opening the door to depression. That usually goes unnoticed.

Always be who you are

I heard "imitation" is a form of flattery. I've seen more people hate and then duplicate. And in my opinion there's really no right or wrong with copying someone's style. But you should give them a shout out. It's the right thing to do. There will be a difference in opinions. With giving a shout out or not. Just stay true to yourself. Everyone has something they admire. Nothing new under the sun. Don't be the last one to know what you truly bring to the table. Go ahead, think out loud.

Speak how you feel. Given it's the right place and the right time. You're not as real as you think you are, if you don't speak on it. There's nothing wrong with expressing yourself. And the best possible way you can. Actually there is a possibility " to ignore it and pay for it". Especially if it's causing stress. Stress is a "killer".

No Controlled laughter

Every smile doesn't equal "peace". Even "laughter" will agree. The words from someone's mouth could choose to tell you anything. Laughter controls facial expressions. Most of the time. If you listen to it, the laughter I'm talking about. You can hear it's intent. Like if it's sinister, or deceiving. But even better if it's happiness. Or joy, pure excitement. You Don't have to look into someone's eyes to tell if you're in the presence of good company. Simple humor can be one way to crack the case wide open.

Cold Game

If the game recognizes the game, be cautious of the games you play. And even more critical of whom you choose to participate with. Sometimes it's a " cold" game. And once you freeze, you're frozen. Making selfish decisions or reckless choices can definitely affect your future. And it's the wrong past decisions coming back to haunt you. No blanket to hide under. Or to keep you warm. Everyone's not playing the same game that you might be playing. Especially if they're naive to it. Once aware of your game. It could be game over immediately. Once the game recognizes the game!

Golden choice

Ok action speaks louder than words. And silence is golden. On one hand, both can be "priceless" but on the other hand, they both can be "costly". There's nothing wrong with showing and proving, but competitive listening, instead of being silent. Your optimism, points to why, what it is you speak of. No matter the value. If you care, a thinking cap is needed. When speaking of taking action. Silent, towards spoken words. Indicates attention. Someone trying to over talk you. Also indicates seeking attention. Don't take this for granted. It could save you a lot of apologizing or frustration. As well as regrets. The correct choices of both. Can be highly appreciated.

In the negative

Being exposed to negativity can lead to speaking and soon living it. It's best to be aware of it. Similar to you seeing a barking dog. Looking to see if the dog has a leash should be your next move. Bad news or negative talk is loud. And can be disturbing. But if no one has any type of complaints about this negativity. You could choose to get used to it. And now you want to rub the negativity on its head. Treating it as if it were a pet.

Corrective vision

I've heard somewhere that you can be diagnosed with what you would call "Rectal Blindness". It's when you really can't see your butt doing that again. Being repetitive is a level of learning. Most people repeat what they already know. Most times unconsciously. Probably a comfort zone. Then on the flip side of it. Some people have the gift to naturally feel disgusted when they have made a life's lesson mistake, definitely if they repeated the same mistake. Bet their asses, become blind to anything that might look to be in relation to what they had to learn the hard way.

Gratification

You should wake up feeling content with yourself, provided that you have enough to get through the day. The Good book says tomorrow brings its " own" worries. Live and be thankful for the day that you have been gifted. I'm quite sure you can find many things to be thankful for. And if you want more abundant things in your life. Get out and get what you deserve. Granted, that it doesn't cost anyone else theirs. Giddy up! You can make an impact in life or lives that you encounter on a daily basis. So be good to yourself. You have things to achieve. But first, Feel the great effects of gratification.

The choice is yours

Everyone is naive to something. But once it's brought to your attention, you're no longer ignorant to that issue. Choices or decisions become available. Sounds easy? Not all the time. Usually it's not as easy as it may sound. But at the end of the day. Choices are provided. At this point are you willing to walk through that door or not? Will you base things on facts? Or are you the type that loves a good mystery? The choice is always yours.

Reflecting on your choices

Great circumstances favors the brave. Even the heart can fail. You should be careful about what you're loving. Your addictions in life really is " your " life. Think about what occupies "You" the most? Is it serving purpose or pleasure? If you're not sure. Try to figure it out. Being organized about it makes a big difference. Are you reaching to grab, so you can eat the fruits of your labor? Or are you craving the sweetest temptations? We usually trust our hearts. So you should be trusting that you can ask your heart hard questions. Such as who and what does it love? If it's necessary. Change your perspective. Can't be lazy and have expectations.

Inspiration comes from observation;

The quality of perception is what could lead to motivation. Meaning everyone gets inspired. A baton is passed all the time. Like in sports. Some will be better, faster, stronger, among you. But that really doesn't matter. It's about being inspired to be the best you can. If you're participating. Someone's always watching. Remember, the ego can be outspoken. To falsely amaze those around you. For its own reasons. But you could be motivating the next best person to step ahead. By passing that baton. Maybe playing a part, in an unspoken plan.

Two faces

We all know someone can have two faces. Be sure that the messenger(s) doesn't throw rocks and hides their hand(s). The enemy could be at their gate. Waiting for the messengers to return. It's natural to fall victim. Being innocent, when negativity is on the move. But more common is to have unspoken enemies. No matter how big or small the situation may seem to you. Pay attention. Did I mention that everyone is not a fan of what you do, or what you have done in this life.

Facts

Advice is really someone's opinion in some cases. If it's not based on facts. It's really what they think of you. Or what they think you are capable of doing. Everyone has different talents. No need to compare to anyone else. You are who you are for a reason. Constructive criticism is okay. Destructive criticism. Sounds like a wrecking ball to your mind. It's meant for destruction. Get out of the way! You can feel whether advice is an opinion or a fact. Like-minded people will cross your path. Keep going until you find an outcome for yourself.

Some days

On those days when I master occupying my time, my views are more vivid. Creative juices flow. The goals you want to accomplish are brewing at that time. Capture the moment. On these days I consider it to be a " Hail Mary " toss" into the in-zone. Doesn't have to be a complete celebration. But like a game, each day can be a win. Celebrated with a good feeling of being productive. I can't speak for you. But days like this come with praise and prayer. Followed by a good night's rest.

What you hear could be distraction

We all hear about rumors of war. Whether nation against nation. Race against race. Even Spiritual warfare. Still, it's a bigger picture. There's casualties from all those wars. But still in my opinion, Keep your faith! "let the dead bury the dead". #Biblical... Keep your eyes on the prize. (A place in heaven). Focus on making better situations. No good deed goes unnoticed. By making a decision to do better as a person, provides better outcomes in your life. Don't worry about the future of he say she say, what will happen in this world. The present time is what we all live in. Remember tomorrow is not promised. Meaning the future isn't either. Be optimistic. Rumors are a distraction of life. Have you been paying attention to something that's more than likely irrelevant to whatever you have going on anyway.

Beware

There's nothing to learn from a person " playing " so-called dumb. That person might be vulnerable or reckless with their way of thinking.(Again be critical of who you choose to play games with) You'll find out the hard way. Self sabotage is common. There could be lots of factors for this behavior. But not a characteristic that's expected of them. When that person truly understands that it's a problem acting unaware of things. Only then, can help be on its way. Playing dumb, could work in someone's favor. In my opinion, if a person is playing dumb, there's nothing to be learned from them. It's a lack of courage. Standing up for what you believe in. They don't really care about respect for themselves. Just dummy their way through life.

Awareness is a must

Try to be aware of your surroundings, no matter where you are or who you're with. You can avoid some things from becoming personal. Trying to fit in is actually a wrong move. You can feel it in your bone structure when you're outta place. Maybe you hear or see it. Don't ignore it. Sometimes this world is very Petty. From the jail cells, you can hear bickering. But the graveyard it's silent, when you're not there. It may sound negative. But that's more than half of reality in this world. Be aware of your reality. Where You are, who you are with. The potential of your safety. And if necessary, an evacuation plan.

Awareness is a must. Part 2

Not approving to alter the mind with alcohol or any other substance. But we all know that most people indulge in the comfort of their own habits. Mostly looking for a good time. To relax or calm their present mood. Could be with the crowd. Could be with close friends, family. Know the vibes regardless. Avoid getting intoxicated with the potentially wicked. It could be a potential birthplace for chaos. Alcohol otherwise known as mixed spirits. Is just what it says. The drink itself. Brings about the spirit of that individual. That's usually dormant. I know you've heard, someone say. He or she is not the same when they are drinking. Again, Be aware of where you are. Who you're with. The potential of your safety. And if necessary, an evacuation plan.

Clown on the stage

I heard in order to fool a fool. You'll have to act a fool. Me, myself, I'm trying not to entertain any foolishness. Being disruptive or putting attention on meaningless stuff are certain people's traits. No one's born this way. It starts in the environment. Some are raised and taught that way. Others are introduced, and adapt to this. And if confronted, maybe depending on your relationship with the person. That person might in secret begin to despise you. Foolishly, you wouldn't have even believed you're a part of the sideshow. Until you're handed the clown shoes. And see the anticipation and smiles of y'all's audience. Are you prepared to be a fool? Or is this a full solo act? You choose to stand in your power. Who really cares if the crowd booed.

Face facts

Certain issues of discrimination such as gender and race will always exist. As long as certain individuals continue to be tardy but request a late pass. Knowing it's time for a change. But doesn't want to be seated before their peers. It has always been an issue. It's powerful in its silence. And strength in it's numbers. Only if there was a scale to view the balance. Everyone knows when it's in play. Very few know if it will end. Or if the ending could ever be in sight.

The Agenda

Almost everyone has tried to justify a wrong doing. And if other opinions are involved, hopefully justice doesn't become blind and false to what's right. Wrongdoing is as silent as a serpent. Justice have to be as Swift as a eagle. Just as in the laws of nature. Will it's prey survive? Whether it's a personal situation. Or a group setting. The outcome changes these people or that person. There's nothing wrong with expressing ourselves. No matter the agreement or disagreement. Until disrespect becomes the agenda. Holding grudges crowds the mind. Leaving no space to resolve the love that once existed. If you're holding dark feelings, that person is also in the dark. Shed some light on the alleged. So things can be seen clearly. That's fair. Also what is considered real.

Believe in yourself

Let those who doubt you, learn something about you. When it comes to life challenges, never let anyone tell you how much motivation is in your Bank. Every champion was once a contender. The spectators are going to spectate. Might even have a commentator. And a few judges, Attending your life's current events. But if they didn't help you get to this fight. Worrying about their thoughts. should be blocked out.Come out swinging. Don't look into the crowd. And Protect yourself at all times. Good luck!

Take care of the love

Where is "love" when you need it? If you have to ask that question, it's not where you're at right now. You can't search for "love". I like to think "love" is similar to the gift of life. Fragile at birth. Needs care and support to grow and become stronger. Also becoming wiser as it blossoms. Learning and some experience will assist in it's growth. Also being aware of who and what could possibly harm it. Should also be a concern. Nurturing like a mother. Protective like a father. If you let love die. No matter the culprit, whether it's abuse, neglect or trust. There's really no way to resuscitate it. Leaving you with the choice of dealing with a "clone" love. Which could never feel the same as the original love. Being considerate of others' feelings can keep a relationship healthy. Just make sure you're receiving the same consideration in full. Think of it as "food for thought". You start to lose weight when you're not eating your share.

Blessing

When someone proclaims to be blessed. Hopefully that person isn't gloating over others' state of condemnation. With boastful intent to make others feel some type of way. Instead praying for you. As well as, the world feels that same vibe. Feeling blessed. Ready to give testimony of their empowerment. Don't look for blessings. Be a blessing. Your rewards become available in your actions. A gesture can always be more positive than negative. Serving your day with pure intentions to help the next person feel loved. It's a combination of both of your days.

Power

D on't believe that anyone is jealous of you for no reason. Some folks are simply jealous of who you are. And money or material things have absolutely nothing to do with it. It's a character. Confidence in who You are. Having the strength to show it at all times. Usually perfect attendance. Standing in your power. Superheroes have alter egos. What makes you think the villain doesn't have alter egos too? You don't need supervision. To see what things are worth. Your brain is all the super power you need. Learn the gifts you possess.

Give thanks

You would probably be surprised if you knew who competes with you while you're just completing your day. What comes naturally to you, others may have to try harder to do so. Be thankful for the skills God has equipped you with. No one wants to be "common". But I would rather have something in common". Especially if they feel the "right " attention is in their presence. If there were a "common" vacancy, right next to you. You can bet they'd be competing with all of their heart to occupy that space.

Surprise test

If it's really all love. For what you decide to put your mind to. Hopefully you can endure painful times. If you're really dedicated, there will be pain in the process. Nothing happens overnight. You will usually have to put in work. The phrase says "live with no regrets' '. Well then how many cares should be given? Depends on how passionate you are about getting whatever it is done. There's different levels of being or feeling content. As well as levels of disappointment when it comes to loving something or even someone. I heard only the strong survive. You'll have to Level up mentally. And stay there. If you're not still elevating to higher grounds. Folding up in the fetal position shouldn't be an option. Love yourself and have an understanding of being tested. For what you really love. This helps set a simple gauge.

Monsters are creations

I've noticed over time that there's such individuals that are down to get into "trouble". But don't want to be in trouble. You can almost always grab your popcorn to see the outcome. Usually they are victims of the monster they created. The loudest in the room is usually the most troubled person. They won't admit it. It took time for these types of individuals to build this character. Thinking this image slows down anything threatening or exposing the comfortability of the identity of their character. Once this monster creates so much confusion. And usually things are out of their control. They'll become victims and ask for mercy. For the monster they created.

What's real

Some people have a misconception of acting or being ignorant, is a reflection of being "real". To me "Real" is being who you are. Mistakes and all. Along with being able to put away your pride if necessary to correct "whatever". If need be. And if somebody is not your " cup of tea" you don't deal with them in any way that would lead them to think otherwise. Unless you need to be professional with them. Having to encounter them frequently. (Co-workers, in-laws, your friends, or siblings. etc). Being civil is a kind gesture. How it was received can only be taken as just that.

Humble enough

All props given to you should be accepted. Especially if You earned them for being yourself. But being humble. And remaining humble is a hard recipe. If you don't know how to check yourself. And some of the worst pies to swallow are "humble pie". It doesn't taste that great. And even more distasteful if you substituted boasting as the crust.

Introducing Jake

Let me tell a brief story about Johnny and his friend Jake. Johnny was what we imagine as a loyal friend. He believed in Jake to be his best friend. They had a lot in common. But also shared different views in life. There were times Johnny would correct Jake when he was wrong. Because that's what a true friend does or should do. Anyways, Jake sometimes would laugh it off. But you'd have to wonder what Jake was really thinking. That's if you knew that side of Jake(Feel me). Johnny didn't really know that side of Jake. That's because Jake didn't want Johnny to know that side. Time goes by. As do different situations. Johnny wasn't perfect. He had his own bag of faults. But even if Jake knew Johnny was wrong, Jake would be silent or afterwards laugh saying " I knew that wasn't right. I just didn't want to say anything". "Cause you know how you can be". Jake would say to Johnny. But actually Jake lived to see Johnny fail or get embarrassed of his dumb actions. The moral of the story, Beware of Jake's around you.

The window

Have you ever given someone good advice? Only to realize the person in the mirror could've used the same constructive information. Thoughts at that time was you were just on the outside looking in. But now you can see your reflection in the window. I know I have. I'm just thinking out loud. Giving you an invitation to know some of my thesis. Reflecting on advice that I have given. Only to realize I could use the same advice for myself in the future. Watching it come back full circle. 360°

Show them

We all know there's no better way to drop science on anyone more than to " show & prove what you're saying". Seeing is believing. Word of mouth can be man's best friend. But that's always pending. To actually have visual to what you're saying is the beginning and end to it. With word of mouth, That dog could be barking at you. Instead of barking for you. So remember to be about it, not talk about it. The respect becomes a different level. Separating the show. And the tickets you are selling.

I am him...Marc d

The "old me" gave birth to the "new me". Even through those labor pains of me growing into the future me, there's appreciation and gratification. Of who I am as a person today. I would like to give "thanks" to the younger me for some of the relationships and goals I kept. Made easier encounters of the future. Folks I haven't seen in years. To see them doing well and to be just living ok, feels good. Loving the moment. Cause I know it has expiration. As do most good times. Other moments arrive, and I remember why I didn't keep in touch with whoever that might be. A simple encounter plays a reminder of who they are to me. And on my end, why we never continue to stay in touch. The old " me" would've given a blunt honest assessment of what I think of the encounter. The "new" me recognizes the good or bad of things. And balance the scale. If no purpose is served. I'll get up from the table. And excuse myself with being humble and leaving in best wishes.

Transformer

Just as everyone experiences life, the good, bad and ugly. You can't change who you are if you don't care to adapt to being a better You. Of course change can be strange. And it's a natural wonder that you have to conquer and adapt to. Life isn't easy. You hear someone say " he or she has changed". It happens to everyone who has chosen to adapt to life situations. Not really the change. But the ability to adapt within the change. They're probably not the same as you remember. Hopefully they receive more blessings than lessons. The world we live in is not perfect. Your personal life is a different story. Who or what narrates your life is actually your personal choice.

Mark, Get set, Goals

Some people's style is just cold beans when you're talking about any kind of goal. Whether it's short or long term. They rather just stick to what they know. Don't let anyone discourage you of what you vision for yourself. They might don't have any direction for their own dreams. Leaving them stagnant. I believe passion has good navigation to the best thoughts. Just know that Doubts could be at every turn. Try not to pick doubts up. Doubt hasn't any directions and has no outlet. So if you're truly trying to achieve goals. You're going to need to bypass most doubts. And this includes people who come with doubts. Whether the outcome is good or bad, You won't feel better until you actually put effort into it.

I am him

Majestic in my way of thinking. I've crossed paths with my weakness in my travels of life. Some I could overcome. Others, I somehow adapted or simply avoided. If you know of me, of course you have an opinion of me. I'm not the type you'll meet and give shrugged shoulders. I've come and I've conquered. Most hardships in my life. Having nothing to do with money or material things. But obtained courage and strength for my soul. Intelligence and wits, knowledge and wisdom wreaking from my brain. Empathy, love and understanding from my heart. Years of experience soaking in what was needed to become who I am today. Let's say I am the "rare one" that cooks til I'm well done. Sincerely Marc d

Useless to testify

Meanwhile, in this world we live in, some people don't talk to you. But they will talk about you to others. It's probably been that way since the beginning of time. I know since I could bear witness to it. Don't be the type of person to deliver gossip to a friend, I personally had to learn this. We all are aware that there's certainly individuals who don't care for you. So why talk about it? Unless that friend has business with whoever in the present or near future that directly affects them. Even then, consider if the message is worthy or meaningful of a positive outcome. If not, Let information wither at your feet where you found it. Don't ride along with anything of irrelevance. Check for purpose. Be that much of a friend.

Time waits for nobody

She was gorgeous, glowing, standing at my door. A total sweetheart . Had this smile with her eyes, matching her pretty lips on a beautiful face. Had to be a heartbreaker. I guess it was just my time. Yeah I saw the signs. But the temptation was easily dominant over my thinking. Flirted with my weaknesses, until my spare time became available to her. I wasn't caught up in my feelings. The situation was straight up with no chaser. I wanted to be there. Our communication was, "what's understood, doesn't have to be explained". If I decided to lay back. She'd fluff my pillow. The smirk on my face was a green light to my soul. And she noticed that there was no traffic. Was she in the right place at the right time? Or were we both victims of attraction? And a fuse had just been lit. I'd look into her eyes and she'd recognize I was there. The reflection that I saw of myself in her eyes was a King. Her beauty to me was custom made for me. I'm talking about every feature of hers was worth smiles. Her personality was best friend qualities. Never thought about trust. Just knew that trust was present with us. I loved her playground. And she'd even take my hand

and show me how she likes to have fun. I loved to play with her. Time was our only interference. In so many ways. Time was the obstacle. Distance, as well as our schedules. Her as a parent, a wonderful mother, a favorite among family. And her family was close. I had my life occupied too. But we had found time together. Those were amazing times. I loved those times. But as time waits for nobody. Time can slowly or quickly change. We've all heard, give it some time. In between time, in the meantime. There's Good times,as well as those ugly times. You might believe in bad or perfect timing. I guess Time is all we have. Wake up to get it right, every single day. Or at least try to understand the time you are giving. It's only to better our lives. Never to make life miserable. Those are the times that we try to escape. One thing for sure though. Time goes on.

Ok with opinions

D id I lose you yet? I know in certain areas. I can get out of reach. Somewhat far out in my way of thinking. But yet and still in sight of an opinion. I would like to think that I'm smarter than most. But more naive than others when it comes to deception. I like to think right about most people. And give them a chance to prove me wrong. I know a couple folks that really prescribe psych meds. Try to say I could use a few scripts. (true story lol). I had to learn to tone down being so outspoken. Even though I'm just thinking out loud. Shaking my head at those that say heaven can be on this cruel earth. That we all share. Actively occupying together. And if you're one of those folks that stays stuck, afraid of your own mind. Suffering from your thoughts, The world only becomes scarier! Avoid this pattern. Train yourself to break free from anything or anyone that restrains you mentally. You'll feel better. Finding out that you're braver than yesterday.

Never pity the fool

I used to not know who to show pity. Even though it was so obvious, I could have heard bells ringing. Instead I'm trying to give my two cents and encouragement to some folks that I thought would be grateful. Not knowing,they were lost. By default. I found them looking for the same encouragement every time we'd cross paths. I've been trying to find my way for years. Looking for that ladder that no one really talks about. But this ladder, everyone knows or will at least hear about it. I've had a blessed but hard life. Never losing faith is a personal victory. I could write a book about it and come back with a sequel. No one stays lost. But for some strange reason some people never want to be found. God bless those people. As well as the babies and fools.

Reduce pricing

Am I my brother's keeper? That was the question that came from the murderer of his own brother. Hate has been around almost as long as love. Which of the two has more value in this world? Love or hate? I really don't know. I would guess hate or being hateful is more common. And in my personal belief. Hate could be more costly than Love. They say Love doesn't cost a thing. Hate is free as well. But once you do a tally, hate can subtract anything you ever built up with love. Even though love is the true reward. Sometimes it's looked at as a trophy, put on a shelf just for whoever sees it to admire. While hate finds its admirers. Producing adrenaline rush. And creating wicked smiles and more.

Think out loud

Go ahead and get judged. Thinking out loud. Just try to be mindful of what comes out of your mouth. Cause in some cases, thinking out loud, speaking wreckless can really make a total mess. On a brighter side, In a few cases, thinking out loud, changed and made way to allow better options, in the way of life so future generations could at least have some opportunities. And survivors or spectators always have their chance to learn from it. We've all witnessed it in history. Great men and women, thinking out loud. I don't have to mention the terrible folks and what they said or have to say. In current or past events. Cause like the skies above, You see them everyday. When you see scattered storm clouds, you find shelter. Treat terrible folks in the same manner. Hopefully terrible folks aren't in your daily travels. At least they don't have to be. Even if they are. Think and speak positively. It can be effective. Remember to do it. Thinking out loud.

Still Marc d

I was born in a small town. Full of flavor and colorful charterers. The cereal city. I've been to other cities and a couple states. But I recognize my swag, it's a part of where I'm from, and I take it wherever I'm at. My style was assembled by my favorite cousins. Slightly modified by my posse in my golden teen-age years. Not perfect by any means. But worthy of anyone's attention when I enter a room. Hate it or love it. If you encounter me in the flesh you'll have an opinion. No doubt. Am I flamboyant? Some of my thoughts can be. Yet I have a private side to me that tries to go unnoticed at times. I know that's easier said than done. Just goes back to being "Worthy" of attention. The right attention or the wrong attention I get it all. Don't judge me until you've had a conversation with me though. It's better when you encounter the Marc d experience.

They don't hide They seek

Some folks seek attention. Whether it's a detailed story. Or those live action go-getters. Retrieving and relaying their actions to say look what happened to me. Ready to perform when there's opportunity for some attention. Ever been given a verbal invitation to the pity party? Social Media can be the biggest host to these events. They have all types of memes for this. No one on the timeline really cares. Not really sure if the person that's delivering care. It's all about the attention they seek. And if you're not listening, they'll find somebody else that will. And if that doesn't work, it's time to log in to social media. Explaining what's on their mind.

100 percent

On a personal note. In these current times in a lot of folks day to day conversation you'll hear them say they're 💯 in every way. But something as simple as cheating on the one they claim to love drops that percentage. I mean if they're willing to dishonor their loved one, loyalty isn't in the conversation. And being 💯 isn't either. There're many examples we can all think of one. Whereas, someone drops their value of being 💯. We all should know that action speaks louder than words. Being loyal is not only a part of being so called 💯. Loyalty as well as honor, respect and trust . A very rare find in people or a person. So what does it really mean to be 100? The answer to me seems to be hard. When so many factors subtract actually being 100.

God first

I remember a friend telling me that the devil tried to kill him in outta town, Mi. He was with a woman, who to him, obviously didn't know God. He never could remember her acknowledgement of God. Whether going through good or bad times. And in the beginning many blessings were there. Of course he would thank God. But the woman would thank him every time. After a while, the little praise the woman was giving him felt good. Gave him what he thought was more confidence, surviving in this world. Even though he would thank God for every goal that was accomplished. He'd loved to hear his woman tell him how he did that. He started to believe her. That he was making things happen. Not that he was blessed by the Almighty. Could this be the devil taking strategic steps to get closer to him? He never really gave that too much thought. He was living well. And was proud of himself and more proud of the props he was given. If you're wondering what happened to him. He learned a valuable lesson. Be humble in the goals you accomplish. Always remember Thank God First and know that you're being blessed. No man or woman alive can bless you more than God's love. Believe that!

Forgive yourself not forget yourself

To forgive is one thing. And to forget is another. To forgive is to move past whatever the situation. But that doesn't mean you can't keep it moving. And have a firm case of rectal blindness.(Can't see your butt doing that again). Depending on the person and situation, of course. To forget is an easy set up for failure. Again depending on the person and situation. To simply forgive has been mistaken for weaknesses. It could be, if what you were taking for granted continues to happen. Appearing in different scenarios. If you find yourself becoming aware of it. Strengthen your values about yourself. Forgive yourself. Don't forget why you're forgiving yourself either. It's all a plan of action. Giving respect to yourself. So the world does too.

My opinion

In my opinion, eventually there comes a time when you don't care what a person has to say about you. Their version of thinking out loud. Your decisions, you live by them. Again be wise but you don't have to honor anybody's opinion except your own. and the Higher powers that be. What's good for you might not necessarily be good for this person who's speaking their opinion. If they're not involved. What you have going on. Keep your thoughts from that person. But never stop thinking out loud. Put those words in the universe and see what comes back that's yours.

Soul food

Funny how someone doesn't realize that they're the source of negative energy. Speaking against your positive Outlook. On guard. Ready to duel. With their verbal sword. It's almost a natural instinct. To accept this verbal battle. Then when you absorb their energy. And they noticed that you have a shield. To deflect their assault. They think it's too much for them! They recognize your power. And will probably go silent. Falling victim in the exact exchange. Becoming a representative. To create class action against you. But where there's truth, no weapon formed against you shall prosper. You were a source of food for their soul. Even if you didn't realize it!

Cake for everyone

Some people can't get used to your status. Their focus is hate towards you. Really a reflection of their own shortcomings or motivation of themselves. Be humble and stand Sampson strong. One day you might have to provide for the same one who hated you! Like I said earlier. Humble pie is hard to swallow! But there's enough cake to pass around to everyone. The person that feels hate towards you. Don't consider this. But if you are the baker. That person can be the candlestick maker. Tell them to get the candles! Cause the cake is done! Best wishes.

Love first

Nothing happens without love! We all know that money is important. We all know that. But love as well as time is precious! Even when people and times change. The memories with those people in those times don't change. Sure as life goes on some things in your past become a blur. But the fondest memories will always attach to you. These memories are a reminder of who that person was to you in those times. That's the power of Love that existed at that moment. If there was a way to go back in time. Everyone feels that they would change certain things. No memories of loss, no feelings of pain. Creating this perfect world of their own. But if everything was perfect. No one would appreciate the true meaning of love.

Knowledge yourself

Make sure that absolutely no one makes themselves relevant to who you are as a person. It's important to know your worth. Self esteem starts with the word self for a reason. There's individuals in society that don't know how to channel their emotions in average situations. In my opinion that's another world crisis! The hurt killing the wounded. Don't be another clown on the stage. If you ever notice, hardly anyone's amused. Unless you're falling down or have a hard time juggling things in life at that moment. Learn to assess the people around you. Stay in the current that flows smoothly in relationships. Anything or anyone stagnant, hasn't anything fresh to offer you. You want to quench your thirst, without the possibility of any negative side effects.

You vs. them

I know this opinion might not fly high. But if they're wishing you hell. You should be wishing them well. Doesn't matter the person, place or thing. Anything or anyone that doesn't mind watching you have problems should be greeted with a plan to say goodbye. And wish them well. Making excuses for them is your love for the devil. A hell you create. But don't know why you're suffering. The situation could be complex. But ask yourself who do you like more? Them vs. You. I'm being fair to them. Is a reflection of being fair to you. There should always be balance.

Do you still know them

Thoughts from last week could change. Due to daily living. No two days are alike. Anyway, if you haven't spoken in a few months or years to someone. You really don't know that person. You have to see if love has stayed present during communications absence. Take no one for granted when it comes to this situation. If you do, The hurt you feel will be self-inflicted. Take this into consideration. Do you feel as if that person really knows you? Things that y'all had in common could have possibly changed. Sure as days, weeks , months, years change. Most of the time people do too.

If they don't know

Staying positive is the struggle in life nowadays. Healing your heart is very important. Surviving and passing through experiences is what helps you decide if you want to aim to be pure. No one, man, woman or child, can love someone all better. It's like a dark room they found themselves in. But they know where everything in the room is placed. Even more important is where's the entrance.   It starts within yourself first. Don't self-sacrifice yourself to make anyone feel love. If they are unable to love you back. Love is giving. But also love is receiving. A mutual unspoken agreement. As I said before, the mouth will tell you anything. Love is mostly taking some kind of action. Creating a sense of security. That you are somebody special.

Growing

Forgiveness doesn't subtract from your life at all. Actually it adds accountability in your future ahead. Being able to move on through mistakes or someone else's mistakes. Forgiveness will set you free. Having the ability to still learn and comprehend future tribulations. You can sit on the shoulders of giants to get further in life. Don't worry about traveling. Sometimes it's about your growth along the way!

Take one for the team

Y ou can't claim to be at peace. When in secret, you worry within. Confidence,Strength as well as Faith are a team. And you need to have them playing for you. Look at it as you're the coach and these are your three Star players in the game. If you want to start winning you definitely have to put them in the game. Your toughest opponent is hate. Known for putting up high numbers. But with practice in true work ethics. You can start to have winning seasons. Have perseverance in your soul!

Noticed

The world has produced individuals that's around you that are more interested in what's going on outside of you. Then what's going on inside of you. If you have the glow. The most troubled people around you notice this. And of course they'll attach to you. With their hidden agendas. You'll have to see and recognize these people for who they are. And exactly what it is about them. That they come around you. If they're not adding to you, they're subtracting from you. Maybe it's your labeling that looks good. Your sauce is original. And they want your recipe! Not to acknowledge and share the love. Only to expose the recipe. Creating an illusion. A false facade. To discredit you. A cowardly nemesis, despising what you're capable of manifesting. If this sounds familiar. Don't be discouraged. Set boundaries. And truly understand that no one can stop what God has planned for you.

Beware when feeding the wild.

Lions, tigers and bears! There's a whole list of dangerous species, including humans. Untamed, once it matures, most likely lives it's life as what we consider to be " wild ". The heart of a predator ignores compassion for its prey! I mean, how can it be rehabilitated of an instinct that has been in place since young? Of course you can show love and compassion. But beware when you're feeding the wild. They're comprehension is different. It's personal survival. Their hunger is real. The outcome to them is the natural laws of nature. Depending on the day. Your presence could be feeding time. It's always a risk that you'll take. When they make an appearance. Or you chose to approach them. Who do you blame? When you have entered or approached the wild. You make it personal. Think about it.

Love doesn't disguise

If you know what love is. Then you know when you're receiving it. Love never comes in a disguise! But hate on the other hand, is a masked crusader. Hate has many identities. Dislike, distaste, despise, detest, loathe etc. The cause of hate could be up for discussion. But why give it that much attention. No spotlight necessary. Recognize hates disguise. Unmasked, it's much more harmless. When you stand over it. Or separate from it. Love has power. Love is Never tainted voluntarily. Deception is a culprit of hate. Testing the strength of love that exists.

Give space

It is said that if you go to a man's house too much. He will learn to hate you. Thin line between love and hate? I don't think so. If there's no common purpose for frequently being in someone's presence. Then uncommon things will become the burden. Could take days, months, weeks, years. Time really doesn't matter, you don't want this to happen. Love isn't crowding someone's space. Love is sharing a space mutually. God blesses the child that has his own. Everyone needs their personal space. Time to time for reflection. Maybe you talk with God. To achieve personal goals. Could be self enjoyment. It's not selfish. It's therapeutic. Also very important, necessary.

Get on that level

It's a cold world without a blanket. Put on your thinking cap. Every action really does have a reaction. Whether it's discussed or not. No one actually knows the depths of someone else's heart. But there's always enlightenment. Whether you like it or not. There's no darkness within truth. So in the choices that you make. Being truthful will be best. For those who can't handle honesty, they are on a different level at the time, about what you have spoken or have spoken. If you're speaking from a loving heart. And that person isn't receptive. How you handle it. It's totally up to you. But the leveling up to the conversation that took place is theirs. Move on for now. Give them time to ponder on what has taken place. Folks timelines are different. We all can be in sync. Have no expectations. Instead have patience. Staying hopeful.

Move around

You can spend time watching a clock. I'm not sure why you would. It's all about what you do with the time in between. Count your blessings! You don't have to be religious to have faith. Religion is man made. God is universal. Use this information as you will. Are you fortunate or unfortunate? Everyday you wake up, it's a chance to do something about it. Gain and maintain. Or complain about everything. You can be the problem. Or choose to solve the problem. Releasing and surrendering to God. Nothing is never hopeless, keep your head up. Stay optimistic. That's the best choice. Brighter days don't have to be a fairy tale. You have to put in the work. In order to witness your dreams become a reality.

Observation

The devil in them. Wanting to attack the God in you! Have you ever felt that way? When everything is peaceful. Your mood is good. You decide to fellowship. And something goes wrong. You can't understand how things went out of course? Could mixed spirits (alcohol) or a type of substance be playing a role. Or just naturally, this person or these people's spirits don't mix? It happens often. No easy fix for this one. Recognize and decide your distance with each situation. The Judge and jury is your gut feeling. Be wise! Don't fool yourself. Whether you know it or not. People will come into your life to fool you. No need to do it yourself. Being able to observe such things as someone's dislike. Could be a lifesaver. It's not being paranoid. It's an indication that pronoia isn't in the building. And you shouldn't be as well. Know your worth. It should be a demonstration for everyone.

Give some room

It might sound repetitive. But understand that some people have a hard time with change. Being patient and giving room for them to alternate within, is helpful. It's an individual choice at some point. Whether to be right or wrong by people. It's ok to compromise. But never make it a total sacrifice for you. Being fair to them. But it's unfair to yourself. You'll be the one with burdens. While the other party aimlessly tries to learn a lesson that's needed.

A look outside the glass

Glass half empty. Or glass half full? Well what if you were to look over the top of the glass? What would you notice? Probably that the glass has enough for you to quench your thirst. Gratitude has almost become an underdog in society. Being ungrateful has spread worldwide like a pandemic. So whether the glass is half empty or half full is irrelevant. Have greater gratitude. That you have a glass with something in it. For if the glass was to spill over. You would immediately understand. Whatever in the glass was still worth it.

Actions versus reaction

B e mindful of bold negative words. Those types of messages are meant for a reaction. However the reaction could be delivered with actions. Which is ultimately the response to those bold negative words. At this point, who was really in control of the outcome? What is the true accomplishment here? There's not a winner. There's not a loser. But for sure, even if unannounced, there's discord. Leading to actions versus reactions.

Problem solving

At times the best repellent in this world, could be expressing your problems or course of tribulations taking place in your life. Life isn't easy. God has a decision to make! Just like you do too. While you're being tested. People in your life are too. If you pay attention closely, you know who passes this imaginary exam to be in your life. And also who has failed. But you have to use logic and a given instinct. Common sense is just that. You're born with it. It's there at all times. Some individuals use it. The unfortunate, leaves this natural Born gift in the corner. And walk out of that room every time. They could care less about using it. Sweeping it under the rug. Thinking everything would just work out itself. Wishful thinking. Instead of a prayer.

Confident

Follow your confidence. Trust who you are. No one in this world can build you up to your superpower. If you believe that someone's validation is your saving grace. You need to change the locks immediately! That someone has your weaknesses in their pockets. So is it best that you distance yourself from pride? I would definitely tell you, definitely! The ego can be shaped so easily. Anyone close enough could damage it. Once the ego is formed completely. It becomes something that could be broken or shattered at any time. Like ceramic or glass objects. Seek and build your confidence for your own good. And stay humble.

Rewards

Celebrations are earned. The work you put in builds your character. Proves dedication, determination and strength in your drive towards the assignment. That you took a part of and conquered. Not everyone will applaud or give praise to your accomplishments. But you're not doing it for everyone. Even if everyone notices. You should no that. Rather than turmoil why anyone does not want to see you shine your light. Because honestly there could be many factors. More than likely you're not one of the factors. Be happy for what you have done yourself. That's the true celebration.

Main event

A true credit of being strong is forgiveness. As I said before, to forgive is a different way than to forget. If you can never find positive encounters in someone's negative face. There's nothing wrong with excusing yourself. Your absence could be affective to that present and future energy. Even if not, you'll find peace in doing so. We all want peace. That's the first step to loving oneself. Finding peace within yourself. To be able to spread peace to someone else. Try it as often as you possibly can. Love won't be far away! Be brave. Be kind. And never be scared to love. It's the main event that God has asked us all to attend.

Knowing this

Once we realize what we are to each other. It'll be easier to recognize what we can truly be to each other. The challenge definitely is to love and nurture what is right. Unchallenging for a fact, is to despise or hate anything or anyone. There's no feeling of gratification. Or something good from hate. More as a dark and cold feeling. That we've all experienced. If you can comprehend what I'm saying. Let's make a change. Put hate in reverse! If you honor the most high. You're trying to save your soul. You can definitely honor him by being a loving person. Save who you can in your life by example of being positive. It's an everyday thing. Not an overnight process. We're human. So everything is a learning experience. What you do with the knowledge that's presented. Will make you wiser in life. Good or bad. Once you know. You know. Be a blessing. It starts within yourself. Your decision.

Villager

I saw it in the community first. Society picks and chooses when and what type of help is given to people. It's said, God bless the child that has its own. Are you depending on someone or something to get you by? There's not a lot wrong with that. As long as there's not any burden for either party involved. Causing possible blame and stereotypes. Making it a task for someone needing whatever could be for resources.

Climb on top of doubts

Appreciate yourself, there's layers of you. Starting with the flesh. Love goes deep within the mind, body and soul. It's all about seeing the truth. Gut feeling or intuition is very real. Spiritual or in denial. You're born with it. That knowing but you doubted yourself more. I warned of doubt before. In my opinion, it's a hellish verb! Meaning doubt could be people, places or things. If what you're planning is realistic. You can climb that distance to see the top of what you believed. How you got there is always the truth to the victory.

Bringing your thoughts to life. Creating a plan. Strategizing and executing the plan. What it took. The dedication of the resources you were blessed with. This is always on the other side of doubts. I told you once again. My part is done with it.

Personalize your victory

Be careful with your planning. It's said, never let the right hand know what the left hand is doing. Everyone isn't a fan of your work. Your calling is a personal victory to achieve. Your friends, family will nonchalantly reveal their feelings towards what you're doing. That will give headway to decide what road you will go down with them. If that's needed. Sometimes they hate be so real. Rather than any love that could ever be shown. They'd rather go silent than give you any admiration. But still, I hope you see them at the finish line helping you celebrate your victory.

Have faith in yourself

Know when you're trying to complete a task, up have faith. And you can't oversee faith, otherwise what would be the point? Be inspired to face the unknown. If it's truly for you. No one has to understand the mission. Put one foot in front of the other. And march to your destiny. Timing is everything. Having faith is a part of strength. In order to live, you have to believe. Anything can be manifested.

Smile

Give yourself a break. Take time to smile. You're always your biggest critic. That's why a positive light is needed. It starts within yourself. You are the chef. Take time for preparation with righteous ingredients. Add love to the recipe. When it's time to serve. If what you serve is good. There will be time for delivery and also take out. Be who you're supposed to be. The world is waiting. Nobody can feel the satisfaction of what you're creating, more than you. Are you going to love yourself? Or let someone else love you more? Make it make sense. I have faith that you got this! Until next time my friends. Take care of yourself. Release the love. And dispose of the hate.

Sincerely yours,

Marcus A. Robinson ♡

CollectKnowledge/GainWisdom

www.ingramcontent.com/pod-product-compliance
Lightning Source LLC
Chambersburg PA
CBHW051546120626
46551CB00013B/1397